JOURNAL AND COLORING BOOK

ESSENCE OF THE TAROT

Modern Reflections on Ancient Wisdom

MEGAN SKINNER

SKINNER PRESS
SEATTLE, WASHINGTON

2021 by Megan Skinner
Published by Skinner Press

All rights reserved. No part of this publication may be reproduced, distributed, or transmitted in any form or by any means, including photocopying, recording, or other electronic or mechanical methods, without the prior written permission of the publisher, except in the case of brief quotations embodied in critical reviews and certain other noncommercial uses permitted by copyright law. For permission requests, write to the publisher, addressed "Attention: Permissions Coordinator," at the address below.

Skinner Press
Seattle Washington
www.meganskinner.com

Ordering Information:
Quantity sales. Special discounts are available on quantity purchases by corporations, associations, and others. For details, contact the publisher at the address above.

Printed in the United States of America

Publisher's Cataloging-in-Publication data
    Megan Skinner, Author.
    Book Title: Essence of the Tarot: Modern Reflections on Ancient Wisdom/Megan Skinner
    p. cm.
    ISBN-13: 978-1-7328894-7-7

1. The main category of the book —Tarot, mysticism, archetypes, intuition, spiritual development. C
HF0000.A0 A00 2010
000.000 00-dc00 0000000000

Second Edition

10 9 8 7 6 5 4 3 2

TABLE OF CONTENTS

BEFORE YOU BEGIN 1

0—THE FOOL 3

I—THE MAGICIAN 11

II—THE HIGH PRIESTESS 19

III—THE EMPRESS 37

IV—THE EMPEROR 35

V—THE HIEROPHANT 43

VI—THE LOVERS 51

VII—THE CHARIOT 59

VIII—STRENGTH 67

IX—THE HERMIT 75

X—THE WHEEL OF FORTUNE 83

XI—JUSTICE 91

XII—THE HANGED MAN 99

XIII—DEATH 107

XIV—TEMPERANCE 115

XV—THE DEVIL 123

XVI—THE TOWER 131

XVII—THE STAR 139

XVIII—THE MOON 147

XIX—THE SUN 155

XX—JUDGMENT 163

XXI—THE WORLD 171

ABOUT THE AUTHOR 179

BEFORE YOU BEGIN

The Essence of the Tarot Journal and Coloring Book uses the *Universal Rider Tarot* deck because the images are traditional and often easiest to understand. However, you can use any Tarot deck you like to work with while creating your Tarot journal.

Here are a few things to keep in mind before you begin:

1. The Major Arcana is the spiritual foundation of the Tarot, and each of the twenty-two cards offers a pathway into understanding your life from a greater perspective.

2. Because the Tarot uses the pictorial language of images, symbols and archetypes, its wisdom is timeless and available to everyone.

3. Your interpretation may be different than what is presented here, and that is the beauty of the Tarot—it is open to individual interpretation, reflecting a meaning that is both universal and unique to you.

4. Although the Tarot can be studied academically, ultimately, understanding the cards is largely an intuitive

process. While using this journal, start with the foundation of the meaning presented, then give yourself free reign to imagine, explore and commune.

5. Take time to create a meditative, sacred space, then either choose a card at random, or select a card that calls to you. Breathe, open your mind and let the Tarot speak to you.

6. Don't over-think it! Your first impression or "hit" is usually right.

7. Journaling your thoughts and impressions about each card is a wonderful way to deepen your Tarot exploration and gain personal insight. If you want more information about a specific situation or dilemma, apply the meaning of the card selected to your question for answers and new perspective.

8. Color your Tarot world! We've included an image of each card for you to color. Coloring helps to open up your imagination and intuitive mind, and can be a meditative experience. There's no rules–just add color in a way that feels right to you. Pull out your gel pins, crayons or magic markers and color away!

0—THE FOOL

Path of: Liberation
Ruler: Uranus
Element: Air

Salvation, whatever salvation may mean, is not to be obtained on any reasonable terms. Reason is an impasse, reason is damnation; only madness, divine madness, offers an issue.
—Aleister Crowley

The Fool wears many faces and may appear to us through a variety of different guises. This is because The Fool is a trickster and a shape-shifter. He is savior, criminal, jester, madman, holy man, and divine child. The Fool exists today in modern playing cards as "The Joker"—the wild card. The Joker can upset a king, trump an ace, and generally cause havoc wherever he appears. The Fool's motto is: expect the unexpected. It would seem only fitting that there is some controversy surrounding The Fool's placement in the Tarot deck. The Fool's number is "0." So does he belong at the beginning, at the end or, as some would profess, between the 20th and 21st Arcanum, between Judgment and The World?

This is an academic argument for which The Fool, in essence, has little inclination. The Fool has no home. He is a nomad, a wandering vagabond, free to travel into our lives when and where we have the need to be liberated from old ways of thinking and being.

Uranus rules The Fool. The connection between the two becomes apparent starting with Uranus' eccentric orbit: revolving around the sun on its side. Uranus represents originality, invention, and independence. This planet serves to awaken us to our creative uniqueness. Uranus is often called "the earthquake planet," and for good reason, as it loves to shake things up and disrupt the status quo. Uranus functions through rebellion. The Fool rebels against all established authority. He obeys a higher order—absolute inspiration—the space where miracles are just waiting to happen.

Before Uranus was discovered (in the late 18th century) the element of Air was attributed to The Fool. The Fool symbolizes pure Air: the realm of ideas and inspiration before they are grounded in time and space. In the realm of Air, all things are possible, and ideas can flourish before they are limited by form. The Fool defies all limitations; he is formless and ever changing. He represents that sublime and blissful state where we are foolish enough to believe in all possibilities.

The Fool's number "0" symbolizes the great void, the cosmic abyss. In this abyss lies all creativity not yet born. To enter this realm and explore its unlimited treasures, The Fool takes on the persona of eternal child. The child is innocent, blissfully unaware of any consequences to his actions or of the future. The Fool appeals to the child within us as all. He represents the folly associated with youth and of the eternal spring. In springtime, we feel free—whether stimulated by nature, or the sheer joy and wonder of discovering the unknown—to act on our most primitive urges. The Fool encourages us to fling ourselves with total and reckless abandon into whatever inspires us in the moment.

A simple definition of this card is *action beyond all reason*. This card can be interpreted in two ways: as a model and as a warning. On one hand, The Fool represents the transcendence of intellect in the name of spirituality or inspiration. Through his ignorance, The Fool becomes divine because in his folly he dares to go where even angels fear to tread. Yet on a practical level, his irresponsible ways make him somewhat of a criminal; his actions are outside of the laws and bounds of normalcy. The Fool walks the fine line between inspiration and insanity. Is he holy man or madman? It is up to you to decide. Crowley says of The Fool: "This queer stranger? Let us entreat him kindly. It may be that we entertain an angel unawares."

Ultimately, The Fool's journey symbolizes the initiate's journey into the Tarot. In a sense, as The Fool travels through the deck, so do you. Those who choose to enter its mysteries are required to be fools, to let go of any and all pretense of reason, to be totally open and fearless to what you may find.

DIVINATION

Look out! If The Fool has appeared to you, be ready to experience profound change. This card represents a quantum leap forward in your life and the beginning of a whole new way of thinking and being. This is a time to be open and spontaneous, to take a vacation from doubt and worry, to play the fool and allow yourself to be and do whatever inspires you in the moment—and damn the consequences! The Fool offers no guarantees, especially in regards to outcomes. Yet, if you dare to embark on his path, to risk his folly, he offers transformation in the sense that you will never be the same again. Have faith. When in doubt or feeling fearful repeat this mantra: "The Fool jumps off the cliff because he knows the angels will catch him. I am The Fool. The Fool jumps off the cliff…"

Q: In what area of your life do you want to take more risks?

> "The Fool jumps off the cliff because he knows the angels will catch him."

Q: What does true freedom mean to you?

_____
_____
_____
_____
_____
_____
_____
_____
_____
_____
_____
_____
_____
_____
_____
_____

> *" He obeys a higher order—absolute inspiration—the space where miracles are waiting to happen."*

I—THE MAGICIAN

Path of: Discipline
Ruler: Mercury

When every cell of your body is so present that it feels vibrant with life, and when you can feel that life every moment as the joy of Being, then it can be said that you are free of time.

—Eckhart Tolle

The Magician is the first card of the deck, and perhaps the most significant, for he holds the key to all of the Tarot's mysteries. Just as the ancient mathematicians (some would call them our first magicians) believed that numbers were sacred and contained the secrets of being, The Magician possesses the formula to the very essence of creation. On a symbolic level, he is the creator; his number is one, representing creative power and the beginning of all manifestation.

Manifestation is a process of sustained effort or energy; it is the will directed towards an intended outcome. For some of us, manifestation does not always come easily, but what The Magician tells us is that it can be learned. Manifestation first requires courage, then effort, concentration, and, a key element to this card, discipline. The Magician is part scientist, part mystic, and part artisan. He takes the potential of The Fool and crafts it diligently and thoughtfully— much as one would solve a math equation, or strive to understand a Buddhist koan (or riddle), or sculpt a piece of clay— into an actual means of expression.

The Magician has been called "Le Batuleur," The Juggler, for he is learning the art of balancing different abilities or tools. The Magician's tools, his instruments of magic, lie on the table before him: a wand, a sword, a cup, and a pentacle. The wand represents desire; the sword, intelligence; the cup, imagination; the pentacle, the physical body, the vessel for manifestation. The tools can be interpreted as different talents or capacities that are in a state of development. We do not see The Magician in the act of juggling for at this moment it is happening solely in his mind. The mind is his learning ground. Because he is able to think it, ultimately, it becomes real.

The Magician's ruler is Mercury, an Air planet symbolizing the mind. In mythology, Mercury is often characterized as a deity with winged feet, here manifested in the lightness of The Magician's being and process. His genius lies in his dexterity. With the concentration of a practiced juggler, The Magician is able to control all the elements and keep them in the air like a juggler's balls, seamlessly, as if there is no beginning and no end. The Magician is joyously at one with his process and, for a moment, he makes us believe that it is easy.

Magicians are masters of illusion. Magic is tricking the mind into a suspension of belief in the properties of time and space. Simply, magic is mind over matter. Some philosophers would tell us that life is an illusion. An ancient Chinese parable beautifully illustrates this concept: "Am I a man dreaming of being a butterfly, or butterfly dreaming of being a man?" It comes down to a matter of perspective. On the Magician's path, we realize the illusion and begin to make it our own.

Astrologically, Mercury rules all forms of communication. The phrase, "in the beginning was the word," is often associated with The Magician, symbolizing the first act of creation. To evoke words, spoken or written, is to transmit energy or ideas into actual form. Mercury is known as the Messenger of the Gods representing the God-given ability within us all to create our lives. Thoughts have power and words are spoken thought. The Magician reminds us that they will greatly shape the reality we experience.

The Buddhist masters speak of Zen as a state of consciousness where one is said to become aware of the infinite possibilities of being, a state that is only achieved by quieting the mind. Consciousness is in the present moment.

Thus said, The Magician can be calculating in his process, which should be used in serving the greater good. All else is deception and manipulation. A simple definition of this card is as above, so below. When we become at one with the eternal flow, we reach a state of conscious fluidity.

DIVINATION

Imagine that there is no past and no future, only now, the present. The ability to fully embody the present moment is the power of The Magician. It is in present time that all true creation begins. This card represents a time of new beginnings, the start of a creative process, or of a new endeavor in your life. You have the tools and may now feel inspired to develop and learn how to use them in a whole new way. This will require letting go of all distractions and focusing on the tasks at hand. Be specific about what you want to create, as your intent is the foundation for all that will become. You're learning as you go, so find joy in the process. Life is your initiation; see through the illusion and recognize your creative power.

Q: What do you want to create next in your life?

> "In the beginner's mind there are many possibilities, but in the expert's, there are few."
> —The Buddha

Q: Where do you need to commit and become more intentional?

"*The Magician's hocus pocus is his ability to focus.*"

Ancient Wisdom—Color the Magician

II—THE HIGH PRIESTESS

Path of: Contemplation
Ruler: The Moon

I early arrived at the insight that when no answer comes from within to the problems and complexities of life, they ultimately mean very little. Outward circumstances are no substitute for inner experience.
—CARL JUNG

Whereas The Magician represented the first step in the act of creation—"I *think* therefore I am," The High Priestess is the second step, the *knowing* of the act. What is the difference between thinking and knowing? It is the difference between light and shadow, reason and faith, words and images; it is the difference between the sun and the moon. The High Priestess is ruled by the Moon. She wears a lunar crown and knows it is in the mystery of the night that her power lies.

The High Priestess is seated and holds an open book upon her lap. Compare her position to that of The Magician, who is pictured standing and looks to be in the middle of a performance. The High Priestess sits passively telling us that, unlike The Magician, there is no action required on her path. If she were to have a task it would be to receive. Perhaps the most difficult of actions is in conscious non-action, in the willingness to sit quietly and to listen. The High Priestess waits in silent expectation to receive her answers as they are revealed from within. She represents the sacred axiom: "Ask and ye shall receive." She has mastered the art of all great mystics, the art of *contemplation*.

The book that has so captured our High Priestess's attention that she seems to be in a state of suspended rapture is the Book of Knowledge (or Secrets). She is the guardian of this sacred book. There are many books of knowledge: the Bible, the Torah, the Koran, the Book of Runes, and the I Ching. The Tarot, with all of its secret teachings and rich imagery, is like a great picture book of knowledge. Pictures and images, unencumbered by the limitations of words, are our purest connection to profound knowledge.

Myrna Lofthus, in her book *A Spiritual Approach to Astrology*, describes the moon as a symbol for "the sum total of all the personalities one has been from previous incarnations." These previous personalities and lives combine in this path to increase our awareness, becoming a multifaceted knowledge. Maybe you have had the sensation of remembering something from another time and place that existed before you were born, or have looked into the eyes of a perfect stranger and felt the eerie chill of recognition, or have had a premonition of something that will happen. Then you have traveled within the timeless domain of The High Priestess. She possesses eternal knowledge: the memory of all things past, present, and future.

The Akashic Records is a theosophical term used to explain this phenomenon. The Akashic Records refers to a universal filing system that is said to record one's every thought, word, and action. These records are impressed on a subtle substance called Akasha, meaning all-pervasive space. Much like cosmic fingerprints or DNA, these records represent the imprint of one's very soul. A simple definition of this card is *intuitive knowing*. Within each of us is knowledge of the potential of all things.

The moon reflects the light of the sun. It represents the earth's soul. When the waters of the moon are stilled, they provide a perfect mirror to reflect our deepest selves, our soul. In traditional astrology, the moon is a symbol for mother. In ancient times, The High Priestess was worshiped as spiritual mother. To the ancient Egyptians, she was Isis, the goddess from whom all Becoming arose. She was the mother of God, the creator of the Divine, and it was through her knowledge that God learned the mysteries of the stars. Yet because of her knowledge and her ability to give life (her feminine power), The High Priestess was seen as threatening to the hierarchy of the male-based church. Often she was labeled crazy, insane, even persecuted as a heretic or witch. Today, The High Priestess, present within all of us, is here to help right the imbalance of male and female in spirituality and religion—to bring the eternal into the present.

In Kabalistic teachings, The High Priestess is represented by the letter Gimel, meaning "camel." This amazing beast has the ability to travel great distances while holding gallons of water in its stomach. There is a tale told about an ancient group of travelers lost in the desert. Desperate and near madness from thirst, they killed their camel and drank the water from its stomach. Are we all not thirsty for water as we journey through this sometimes desert wasteland of life? The High Priestess represents a well for us to drink from, that of the great eternal ocean known as the soul.

DIVINATION

This is a time to go within and nurture your soul through meditation and deep contemplation. You may find yourself experiencing a heightened state of awareness, in touch with a consciousness that is an extension of your present reality. Remember, the intuitive realm does not always line up in a linear manner; it is an extra fold of perception. Trust your senses, your feelings, and your intuitions, whatever comes to you in the moment. Let them reveal to you what you need to know. Breathe through each moment with its gift of reflection. You are in a process of "deep remembering." If your sense of memory brings you sadness, it may be that you are experiencing an "eternal sadness." Blessed are those with the gift to cry. Cry the tears of the moon.

Q: Are you allowing time to commune with your deeper soul energies?

_____
_____
_____
_____
_____
_____
_____

" She has mastered the art of all great mystics, the art of contemplation."

_____
_____
_____
_____
_____
_____
_____

Q: Do you own and celebrate your intuitive wisdom?

___

"*Bringing the eternal into the present.*"

Ancient Wisdom—Color the High Priestess

III—THE EMPRESS

Path of: Love
Ruler: Venus

True love is nothing but a certain urge striving to fly up to the divine beauty.
—Marsilio Ficino

The Empress is one of the most popular cards of the Tarot deck. Like her ruler Venus—a planet so brilliant that it is often called a star—The Empress radiates a luminous intelligence, and we cannot help but be dazzled by her light. The Empress wears not so much a crown as a tiara of jewels or stars representing the twelve stars of creation or the twelve signs of the Zodiac.

Venus is the planet that inspired the childhood rhyme: "Star light, star bright, first star I see tonight. I wish I may, I wish I might, get the wish I wish tonight." The Empress inspires our wishes, our desires, and the promise of all creativity.

In astrology, Venus rules two signs: Libra and Taurus. Libra represents the airy qualities of this planet, our ideals of beauty and love. Taurus, the earthy aspect of Venus, epitomizes the sensual and tactile. Libra appreciates beauty intellectually, like a connoisseur discussing fine art. Taurus is more Bacchus-like: a fabulous dinner party with good food, good friends, and lots of wine. The Empress incorporates the Venusian qualities of both signs—the rational and the passionate; it is the principle of pleasure in all its forms.

In Greek mythology, Venus is known as Aphrodite, the Goddess of Love and Beauty, who enticed both men and gods alike. Venus and The Empress relate to the archetype of Eve in the Garden of Eden. Eve was sublimely naughty. She conversed with the Serpent, ate the "forbidden fruit," and tempted Adam. The Empress is confident in her sensuality, her ability to give life. She is open and welcoming and feels no need to protect herself.

The Empress also represents mother, or motherhood, a creative process in itself. The Empress is the earth mother, as compared with The High Priestess, the spiritual mother of the Tarot. Both cards represent the feminine, but each is different in its expression. The High Priestess fits the image of the Madonna: virginal and enigmatic. The High Priestess looks rather austere, even intimidating, her consciousness pristine and, in a sense, untouched. She has chosen the Veil of Isis, a cloak of mystery to protect herself.

The Empress card as a symbol of motherhood may translate to relationships with our own mothers. This relationship is our first experience of the feminine. In a psychological sense, the mother relationship is the most primal and complex of all. It affects the quality of all our future relationships, greatly shaping our ability to love both others and ourselves.

Traditionally, the mother is the nurturer, the giver of comfort, love, and support. In the purest sense, The Empress represents unconditional love, the highest of all love, given without expectations. When out of balance, The Empress can be an over-protective and possessive mother, an over-giver. For some, The Empress may represent our mothers' unfulfilled desires.

A simple definition of this card is the *wisdom of love*. Through this path, we explore our capacity to give and receive love. This process involves learning a balance between heart and mind, a balance of self and other. Ultimately, The Empress represents the capacity to nurture and support us in equal proportion to the ability to nurture and support others.

The Empress could be described in terms fitting the quality of a Renaissance painting. The Renaissance was a time when astrology and the arts flourished, where artists and philosophers looked to the heavens and the celestial bodies for insights into the human condition. The artist Sandro Botticelli was an individual inspired by the spirit of Venus. Indeed, the Goddess of Love became his muse. Botticelli's paintings show voluptuous women, often naked, frolicking in nature and the elements. The Empress is a sensual celebration of nature and of life. She is comfortable in her body, for it is in her body that she experiences love's many pleasures.

The Empress then is love, in regard to both its celestial and terrestrial aspects. Her number is three, representing body, mind, and spirit. Here, the path to the Divine is through the gift of the body: Where love and desire become art itself.

DIVINATION

The light of love shines brightly within you. As you become more comfortable with yourself and your life, your confidence will attract others to you. You deserve love but you must decide what quality of love you wish to receive. Enlightenment comes from a feminine wisdom, the ability to make wise choices. This is a time to take a step back from the "busy-ness" of life: Stop and smell the roses and experience all that you have created. Be proud of your creations, no matter how big or small. They are like flowers in a garden and, with love, they will blossom and grow. Nurture yourself, your body, and your senses. For now, pleasure is not a luxury, it is a necessity. Love is all around you, so partake generously, and then abundance in all its many forms will surely follow.

Q: What is your relationship with beauty and pleasure?

> "The Empress also represents mother, or motherhood, a creative process within itself."

Q: What does unconditional love mean to you?

> *Star light, star bright, The first star I see tonight. I wish I may, I wish I might, Have the wish I wish tonight."*
> *— Roud Folk Song*

Ancient Wisdom—Color the Ancient Wisdom—Journal the Empress

IV—THE EMPEROR

Path of: Authority
Ruler: Aries

We should conduct our lives as though we were kings and queens with all eternity before us.
—Eliphas Levi

The Emperor's path is a majestic one, as well it should be, for here we become symbolic kings, the masters of our domain. Yet it is not always easy to be king. The Emperor wears a heavy crown, representing *authority*, and with it, the burden of responsibility. Authority is a divine right; how we choose to deal with it is another matter. At his best, The Emperor is a powerful ruler, a leader who acts with the greater good of the kingdom in mind. When out of balance, he becomes domineering, controlling, and authoritarian—a tyrant.

Aries, a Fire sign and the first sign of the Zodiac, rules The Emperor card. Aries implies *beginnings*, symbolizing the assertion of the individual ego (fire) as it strives to separate from source. Mars, the mythological "God of War," in turn rules Aries, here fighting against the collective pull of the past and helping us to individuate. The Emperor is the archetype of warrior. He is the original warrior engaged in the ultimate battle—the battle to be.

In astrology, Mars is the masculine principal, male energy, representing the urge for action, the desire to create self. The Emperor, potent and all-powerful, is pure male energy. We all have a male and female side, not necessarily in a sexual sense, but in regards to our larger psyche. The Emperor card symbolizes the way in which we express our male energy.

Robert Wang defers to the wisdom of the *Golden Dawn* text in his description of The Emperor as "the general, the conqueror, hot, passionate, impetuous." In history, we have many examples of the warrior/emperor's dark side, namely of his abuse of power and his aggression. The Roman Empire was built (and destroyed) during the astrological period of Aries. The Emperor Napoleon is a classic example of warrior-energy run a muck. His was a case of conquering for the sake of conquering, where the need for ego gratification overtook wisdom and reason. This is a tradition that unfortunately continues in the world today.

Yet the emperor we see here holds no weapon. He is not going into battle. This emperor is seated on a stately throne of granite or stone, on solid ground. He does not rule by the sword, but by his scepter—a crucial distinction. His scepter, like his crown, represents authority. The Emperor is an imposing figure: regal, powerful, and dynamic. He has earned his power and, most importantly, he has owned the responsibility of it. It is through this ownership that others naturally respect and respond to him. He rules, not through force, but by the sheer nature of his presence. Here we learn the fine art of governing and keeping the peace, of how to lay down the law and set clear boundaries, even if becoming a leader means that you will displease some.

The Emperor is also a symbol of our paternal role model. In a psychological sense, "father" represents how we make our way in the external world, the world of form. The Emperor represents the ancient rite of passage from father to son (or daughter) where we become responsible for not only our lives, but the lives of others as well. A simple definition of this card is personal sovereignty. In dignifying self, you give dignity to others. Authority requires discipline, assertiveness, patience, and teamwork. By adhering to these qualities, you become worthy of wearing The Emperor's crown.

The Emperor's number (four) represents *foundations*. On this path, we create the foundations for our "kingdoms," our business empires, which we will build into careers. This is an excellent time for conquering new business enterprises. In these endeavors, The Emperor is energetic and forceful while at the same time providing a stabilizing influence. This requires an instinct for knowing when to act and when not to act—the mark of true leadership.

DIVINATION

You have reached an auspicious moment in your life. This is the time where you take to your throne of personal empowerment. How you conduct yourself now is of great importance; others are looking to you for leadership. Act with integrity toward yourself and others. Issues may now arise with males in your life, specifically authority figures: your father, mentor, partner, or boss. This is a circumstance where you may feel someone is trying to dominate you, or you have to defend your turf. However, this is not a time for battle. Do not act impetuously. Take a step back, center yourself, and remember that if you are truly powerful, no one can take it away from you. New enterprises in business thrive, as you are full of energy to create your kingdom. You are laying important foundations for the future. Pay careful attention to follow-through.

Q: What does power and authority mean to you?

> "Remember that if you are truly powerful, no one can take that away from you."

Q: Are you the confident master of your destiny?

> "*Authority is a Divine Right; how we choose to deal with it is another matter.*"

Ancient Wisdom—Color the Emperor

V—THE HIEROPHANT

Path of: Divinity
Ruler: Taurus

When leading, be generous with the community, honorable in action, sincere in your words. As for the rest, do not be concerned.

—The Buddha

The Tarot has survived many incarnations and variations, according to the current historical and political climates. In olden times, often the only way to pursue one's mystical nature was through the sanctuary of church. Hence, many of our greatest esoterics and mystics were Catholic priests. In fact, in some decks The Hierophant is known as "The Pope." Before the rise of Christianity, "Hierophant" (Reveler of Sacred Things), was the distinction given to the High Priest of the Eleusian Mysteries. Whatever his title, the figure portrayed in this card represents a seemingly infallible presence. He is a leader and a shepherd of Divine law.

The Hierophant is shown in the act of benediction: the giving of divine blessings. He represents our earthly connection to higher spheres, to heaven and God itself. The Hierophant is a conduit, the intermediary between the human and the Divine. He is the embodiment of spiritual father, the person or authority whom we trust with spiritual matters and the keeping and well-being of our soul.

"Father, pray for me." To minister to the soul of another is both an awesome and daunting responsibility. The previous card, The Emperor, also represents father. Through the emperor/father, we mastered authority and its natural expression of leadership. In The Hierophant, we take leadership to the next level—the ability to influence and advise others on their spiritual journey. The Hierophant could be summarized in this way: the recognition of one's worldly spiritual power and the desire to express it externally.

A simple definition of this card is: *Spiritual Teacher*. Throughout the ages, there has been a tendency to put our spiritual leaders on a pedestal. This is to assume that they are somehow above us. This practice has nothing to do with spiritual empowerment. Instead, it becomes a turning over of one's own individual power in a misguided attempt to connect with the Divine. Any spiritual authority, no matter how elevated, is by the very nature of his (or her) incarnation still human and still fallible.

This path challenges our beliefs and ideals about those we trust and look to for spiritual guidance. It warns us to watch for false prophets and teachers and reminds us not to surrender our individual power. As Liz Simpson states in *The Book of Chakra Healing*, "a spiritual teacher is not a human being trying to be spiritual, but a spiritual being learning vital emotional lessons by wearing the cloak of humanity." A spiritual teacher is learning the lessons of divinity though the conscious experience of finding the sacred in everyday life and in everyone.

The Hierophant is a communion between the individual and the Divine; it is the relinquishing of individual will to Divine will. Divine will is a detachment from outcomes, the willingness to surrender a situation or problem to a higher power. Here we sacrifice ego to become an empty vessel pure of agendas and expectations. As we let go of material concerns and become empty and open, we are in a position to receive spiritual abundance. The gifts of spirit are rich and plentiful. Here we learn the true meaning of value, the sense of security that comes from an active communion with spirit.

Taurus, an Earth sign, rules The Hierophant card. The element of Earth represents the physical-material plane, specifically the body. The Hierophant signifies the point where spirit becomes flesh: the unification of body, mind, and spirit. This is a union in search of a beloved and a fitting prelude to the next Arcanum, The Lovers. On a mundane level, this card can translate to the union with another and may present itself when one is contemplating sacred vows and contracts, such as marriage.

Taurus is a fixed sign: conservative, traditional, and above all else, stable. Here, it translates to an enduring and rock-solid spiritual foundation we can count on. It is our church, fulfilling our need to belong and ground with others in the pursuit and exploration of a connection to the Divine.

DIVINATION

We all have the potential to be spiritual teachers, and this path may take many different forms. Sometimes being a spiritual teacher simply involves having an open heart and an open mind, and the willingness to acknowledge someone else's journey without judgment. You should strive to make even the most trivial encounter a positive learning experience. In the process, you will find that you receive as much as you give. This is spiritual abundance. Now is a time where you are seeking a connection with your spiritual community, an extended spiritual family where you can share ideas and celebrate the gifts of spirit. Know that your good intentions for others are greatly appreciated and engage the spirit in a way that is prosperous for all.

Q: What is your concept of a spiritual authority/teacher?

> "A spiritual teacher is not a human being trying to be spiritual, but a spiritual being learning vital emotional lessons by wearing the cloak of humanity."
> —Liz Simpson

Q: How can you embody a more spiritual life?

" The gifts of spirit are rich and plentiful."

Ancient Wisdom—Color the Hierophant

VI—THE LOVERS

Path of: Discernment
Ruler: Gemini

In this house of mud and water, my heart has fallen into ruins. Enter this house, my Love, or let me leave.
—Rumi

Alas, this is not a particularly romantic card. Such sentiments are perhaps better left to the Venus-ruled Empress, the path where love and desire meet. Gemini, an Air sign, rules The Lovers card. The element of Air can be cold, for here it represents the realm of the mind and the intellect. It is through the airy qualities of Gemini that we begin to form our ability to reason, to make distinctions and discriminate between right and wrong. Thus The Lovers represents the process of gaining discernment in your relationships.

A simple definition for The Lovers is *choice*. Typically, this card means a reality check in a relationship where a decision must be made, a choice that will greatly determine the outcome of the situation.

The story of Adam and Eve in the Garden of Eden is an obvious archetype for The Lovers. In Adam and Eve we have our first lovers and, most importantly, the first choice—paradise or sin? It is the eating of the forbidden apple, the fruit from the *Tree of Knowledge of Good and Evil* that causes the lovers to be cast out of paradise. Once they tasted the fruit, in a sense, they knew too much. It was through their awakened desire for experience that they became conscious of their nakedness, and thus their vulnerability.

We may all wish for the blissful Eden-like innocence of romantic love. Yet in romantic or idealized love there is little room for growth and learning, and The Lovers card is all about learning. This path signifies relationships, or the prospects thereof, which offer a universal, albeit sometimes painful, learning experience. In relationships, we become open and vulnerable to another—a scary proposition at times. The hook that keeps us there moment to moment, day to day, through the most difficult of lessons, is love.

Without this vital, often mysterious, sometimes perplexing feeling called love, we would likely throw up our hands and abandon the whole enterprise.

What is love? Astrologer Richard Idemon describes it as "a force that brings two or more separate entities together in a way that they are totally transformed." Eros is deep and passionate love—a creative force. Through Eros we create life. And in its presence, from the heights of intimacy to the lows of longing and despair, we are transformed.

In Greek mythology, Eros is also known as Cupid, the son of Aphrodite (or Venus) who is the Goddess of Love. Cupid is a mischievous god, a trickster who shoots his arrows into the most unsuspecting of victims sending them into total disarray. Cupid may seem to strike at random, without reason, but when associated with The Lovers, we can see some purpose to his schemes. Gemini is a sign of *duality*, symbolized by the twins. Here, the rules of attraction apply. Gemini represents the exploration of self through other—the mirror of a relationship. In psychological terms this can be explained as projection, which is the projecting of one's missing self, one's unfulfilled needs and desires, onto another. Today's popular notion of finding that elusive soul mate is perhaps in reality a search for our other half, a cry for recognition, a disguised yearning for wholeness.

Commitment is not the natural forte of notoriously fickle, ever curious Gemini. Indeed, this is often a life path issue for this sign. But a relationship, at least the deep transformative variety, requires commitment. This being a card of growth and learning, the idea of true spiritual marriage is most appropriate here. To the mystics, The Lovers card represents the alchemical marriage, a union with self that progresses into a relationship with another.

Ultimately, by being complete within one's self, we are free to enter into the unknown abyss of love and be transformed in the process.

True union is a responsibility and a commitment—what happens after the honeymoon and beyond the fairy tale with all of its romantic trappings. This requires a letting go of the need for perfection or any attachment to outcome. Although challenging, this path offers the promise of great learning and the opportunity for deep personal realization. In the highest sense, the choice offered in The Lovers will bring one back to oneself. For it is rightly said that you can only love another to the degree that you love yourself.

DIVINATION

You stand at a crossroads and a choice is before you regarding a significant relationship in your life. Think carefully. That which attracts you to another holds a magnificent reflection of your deepest desires. Do not doubt yourself. As difficult as it may be, try not to let past emotions or sentiment sway you. You must commit one way or another. Pain comes from indecisiveness. By making up your mind, you will set your heart free. Remember, there are no wrong choices, only learning experiences. Whatever your decision, know that the journey ahead will lead you to a place of greater understanding and wisdom about yourself. If you are presently unattached, you are now opening yourself up to the grand adventure of falling in love! Write down what you wish to experience with another—then let it go.

Q: Are you willing to fully commit in your relationship?

" *You stand at a crossroads, and a choice is before you.*"

Q: In which relationships do you need to be more discerning?

" *You can only love another, to the degree you love yourself.*"

Ancient Wisdom—Color the Lovers

VII—THE CHARIOT

Path of: Achievement
Ruler: Cancer

Everything in the unconscious seeks outward manifestation, and the personality too desires to evolve out of its unconscious conditions and to experience itself as whole.

—Carl Jung

Cancer, a Water sign and the astrological ruler for the moon, rules The Chariot card. Moon and Water are elements associated with the unconscious. What does the unconscious have to do with the proud young hero we see pictured here, poised at the helm of his mighty chariot? A definition may be helpful. According to Webster, the unconscious is, "the part of the mind containing the psychic material of which the ego is unaware… not deliberately planned, organized or carried out." One could think about The Chariot as Cancer, the crab, emerging from the great ocean onto solid land, a process where the unconscious becomes tangible and real. This card represents your dreams becoming reality.

On a mundane level, Cancer represents home. When considered more deeply, this translates to the *home within*, the security that comes from being "at home" and comfortable with yourself. The task at hand is to take this sense of authentic self, your mobile home, into the outer world. To do this successfully, one's personal and emotional house must be in order. The crab's shell serves to protect it from outside forces and influences.

On this path, we gain a deeper sense of identity so as not to be thrown by the whims of others. Here we learn to be in charge of our journey. More than anything else, The Chariot is a test of character. Here we meet our hero, the symbolic hero that lies within us all. Joseph Campbell describes the hero's journey as a series of courageous acts, a continual process of trials and triumphs, which offer a life lived through self-discovery. The Chariot presents a challenge and an opportunity to define one's true self and character, a noble and heroic effort. The traditional meanings associated with this card, of victory and success, refer to a triumph of personal integrity in the face of unknown elements or adversity. "To thine own self be true" is a fitting motto for The Chariot.

In esoteric astrology, Cancer symbolizes the soul's point of entry into the body, the doorway into incarnation. In The Chariot is an implied birth, a new beginning, or at the very least, a turning point in one's life. This card potentiates a breakthrough of the psychic self—the inner unknown engaging with the outer world, a movement of the soul. The Chariot is the vehicle for this passage, much as the body serves as the vehicle for the expression of one's soul.

Cancer is the second cardinal sign of the Zodiac. Its cardinal qualities are personal, creative, assertive, and forward moving. The cardinal forces drive The Chariot to conquer new levels of individual achievement. We encountered the first of the cardinal signs in The Emperor (Aries), representing the path of authority. The foundation of personal authority established through The Emperor makes the journey of the Chariot possible. Without the ability to dictate one's own needs and desires, the adventure ahead would be fraught with much peril.

In closing, we end where we began, with Carl Jung. The Chariot's journey closely resembles what Jung described as the process of individuation, a process of uncovering the true self. Jung states that consciousness comes from the unconscious, and ultimately, that the whole person is a collaboration of the two. The crab is an amphibious creature; it can exist on both water and land. The wholeness of which Jung speaks is meaningful here as it symbolizes the unification of one's physical and spiritual worlds, a beginning and a completion. A simple definition of this card is *acting on intuition*.

DIVINATION

Congratulations! Much inner-work has been done laying the foundation for a triumphant move forward. Plans previously stalled or waylaid can now be set into motion. The journey ahead will take you to many exciting new places and situations, and this in itself will challenge you. You are leaving much behind, but past experience will serve you well. You are the hero of this campaign; stand tall and do not look outside of yourself for validation or applause. If you feel the need to prove anything, then it is only to yourself. Glory comes from within. Although outcomes are not the focus here, all indications point to success in new endeavors. There is no game plan, for it would only limit you. When uncertain, take a step back and reconnect to the deep reservoir of your spirit for guidance.

Ancient Wisdom—Journal the Chariot

Q: What dream are you wanting to manifest?

_____
_____
_____
_____
_____
_____
_____
_____

"*To thine own self be true.*"
—*Shakespeare, Hamlet*

_____
_____
_____
_____
_____
_____

Essence of the Tarot Journal and Coloring Book

Q: Do you trust your intuition to guide you on this journey?

_____

_____

_____

_____

_____

_____

_____

_____

_____

_____

_____

> "The Heros' journey is a continual process of trails and triumphs…offering a life lived through self-discovery."
> —Joseph Campbell

_____

_____

_____

_____

Ancient Wisdom—Color the Chariot

VIII—STRENGTH
Path of: The Heart
Ruler: Leo

And there the lions ruddy eyes, Shall flow with tears of gold: And pitying the tender cries, And walking round the fold: Saying; wrath by his meekness And by his health, sickness, Is driven away, From our immortal day.

—William Blake

Each card of the Tarot tells a story. The story of the Strength card is *The Virgin and the Lion.* There are many variations of this timeless tale, including Aesop's fable of "The Lion and the Mouse," but perhaps the most popular version of this story is "The Beauty and The Beast." A story that goes something like this…

Once upon a time, there lived a fair maiden, here called Virgo, the innocent. One day she met a ferocious beast—a lion. The maiden was both attracted to the great beast and afraid of him at the same time. She asked herself many questions. Should she run away? Call for help to cage the beast or put him into chains? She contemplated killing the lion, but like all great stories, this is a love story, and Virgo, with her virginal gift of innocence, believed she could tame the beast and become his friend.

The Strength card is known by several names. In some decks it is called "Force," in the Crowley deck, "Lust." The lion pictured in this card is opening his mouth to the maiden Virgo. This opening, or surrender, does not happen through brute force. She is not physically capable of such an act of strength.

The heroine of our story has a compassionate heart. She is willing to believe in what others would not, namely in the lion's inherent goodness. She acts with mercy. Her patience allows her the time to know and understand the lion. Through this willingness the maiden finds herself falling in love with the fearsome creature. The result is a miracle: Virgo's love transforms the lion. Against all odds, he yields to her, without effort or struggle. This card recognizes the power of gentle strength. This is a strength that can move mountains.

The lion represents our primal animal nature. He is a symbol of passion and desire, the beast within, what we lust for. (We will meet the inner beast again in the path of "The Devil.") For many of us, lust and desire are not always comfortable feelings, often having negative associations. Yet desire is the first step in any creative process. Desire activates the vital life energy, the sacred fire, what is called the Kundalini energy or the "serpent power." This powerful force represents an initiation, unleashing our creative, psychic energy. If, like the maiden, we can learn how to cooperate with the "serpent-beast," we can reach a state of peace with ourselves.

A simple definition of this card is *kindness*. Strength comes from union, the union of mercy and desire. If you fear your passion, it will consume you much as a lion would devour a lamb. The Strength card is the path of the heart. It requires a loving act of self-acceptance. Embrace yourself, warts, fangs, claws, all of you—even the seemingly undesirable or imperfect parts.

The Strength card is ruled by Leo, the beast in our story. Leo, a Fire sign, governs the heart. The heart pumps blood, vital fluid and the energy of life, through the body. It is the source of our creative fire: what we love, our passion, what makes our heart beat fast to a timeless rhythm. Yet from an early age, many of us have been lead to believe that our desires are inappropriate or even bad. This type of conditioning takes away our creative power. The lion's fierceness comes from a wounded heart, a sense of powerlessness. This brings us to the moral of this story: Become one with your heart's desire, and like the maiden and the lion, you too will be transformed.

DIVINATION

Have you been avoiding yourself? Perhaps you are experiencing an inner struggle, a conflict with self that makes you feel weak. The physical manifestation can be exhaustion, weariness with life. The remedy is to make peace with yourself, all of yourself. Do not force anything. Instead, be gentle and patient with yourself. Allow yourself to be vulnerable. Vulnerability is not a sign of weakness. In genuine vulnerability you will find your greatest strengths. Spend time reacquainting yourself with your passions, needs, wants, and desires. It is okay to be self-full, which is different from selfish. To facilitate your own unique process, begin to contemplate what you want in your life. This may mean lifestyle changes, as you search for a quality of life that brings you the deep satisfaction and contentment that you deserve.

Ancient Wisdom—Journal Strength

Q: What is your relationship with desire?

" *Desire is the first step in any creative process.*"

Q: What parts of yourself do you need to accept and love unconditionally?

_____

_____

_____

_____

_____

_____

_____

_____

_____

> *"In genuine vulnerability you will find your greatest strengths."*

_____

_____

_____

_____

Ancient Wisdom—Color Strength

IX—THE HERMIT

Path of: Wisdom
Ruler: Virgo

Yea, though I walk through the valley of the shadow of death, I will fear no evil; for thou art with me; thy rod and thy staff they comfort me.

—23rd Psalm of David

We begin The Hermit with a prayer, the invoking of the Psalm 23. The Hermit shown here *seems* very much alone, but remember, as you embark on this path: One never prays alone. The Hermit card presents a mysterious figure shrouded in a dark cloak. The cloak conceals The Hermit, making him somewhat invisible, and merging him with the dark night in which he travels. It is as if he is saying, "I am the night," telling us that he has not only accepted his journey, but also embraced it. He has only a single lantern to light his way in the darkness.

The symbolism here is plentiful. The cloak renders him separate and alone, in a sense, unreachable. His staff is a symbol of wisdom and intuition. Though he may not be aware, it directs The Hermit's course. The darkness represents his journey into the inner reaches of the unknown. Yet it is the lantern that is perhaps most significant to The Hermit's path. The lantern represents his faith, defined as a belief or calling to something greater than self and circumstance. Without faith, he would truly be alone. It is the light of The Hermit's lantern that both guides and comforts him on his long journey.

The astrological ruler for The Hermit is Virgo, an Earth sign. Virgo's birthday falls in the last days of summer, a time traditionally associated with the harvest, when we reap the hard labor of summer's seeds sown. The symbol for Virgo is the virgin, suggesting purity and innocence. Virgo represents the "virgin soil," the fertile ground from which wisdom is born.

The Hermit is a seeker of knowledge and wisdom. Knowledge and wisdom are two very different things. Knowledge comes from books, whereas wisdom must come from the heart. Thus the road to wisdom can be a difficult path, for true wisdom is only attained through the hard lessons and experience of time. With the virgin's purity often comes a need for perfection, hence Virgo's tendency for over-analyzing and self-criticism. But here we must rise above such tendencies to plant our seeds and trust that through patience, love, and proper nurturing, they will grow. Incidentally, these are the very lessons of the preceding "Strength" card.

This is not hope; hope is for the young and the impatient. Wisdom requires vigilance. It is a constant act of faith. The Hermit knows this, for he is wise beyond his years. He is the embodiment of an old soul.

Throughout history there have been many legends of wise souls, masters and teachers like The Hermit. One is that of the mythological wizard Merlin who guided young King Arthur to the throne of Camelot. Those familiar with the Merlin saga know him not only as a magician, but an architect, prophet, bard, and healer. Merlin followed the "old ways" of the ancient pagan or Druid sects that worshiped the Goddess and the earth. Merlin possessed many gifts, perhaps most notably his ability to connect to, and understand, the magic inherent within nature.

Both Merlin and The Hermit share a desire to serve, to help and mentor others through their own difficult processes. Hermits like Merlin work behind the scenes, sharing their knowledge, without glory, for a higher purpose, appearing to their young protégés from the shadows in times of their greatest need.

In hermetic teachings, The Hermit was one of the three Wise Men who followed the Star of David (or Bethlehem) to the manger of the Christ child. Some biblical scholars say that these wise men were actually Persian priests or magicians, likely astrologers, who divined through the placement of the stars the coming of this miraculous event. The Hermit represents the use of knowledge merged with the power of faith, a heady combination.

A simple definition of this card is a *test of faith*. Generally, this path represents a trial of one sort or another, a test of your beliefs in yourself, others, and the greater good. The Hermit's journey is a lonely one fraught with many perils, the most prevalent being isolation and despair, a feeling of being forsaken by God. True wisdom must come from within, from experience and an inner sense of knowing. By enduring the rigors of The Hermit's path, he offers the richest of rewards, the peace that comes from internal fulfillment.

DIVINATION

If you are feeling lost or alone, do not despair. It is only by traveling into the darkness of the unknown that you will find the answers you seek. Cultivate and guard preciously your alone time. Fortify yourself with the wise counsel of those masters who have walked before you. There are teachers all around you, and guidance may come in unexpected ways—from the passage of a book, a chance meeting with a learned friend, or even in the subtle nuances of a song's refrain. You may find that you are inspired to learn and educate yourself as a way of developing your inner talents and gifts. If you have chosen this card, you have the ability to guide or serve others in some way, a worthy path. For now you don't have to share or explain your process. The Wise Man keeps his own counsel.

Ancient Wisdom—Journal the Hermit

Q: What is the difference between being alone and loneliness?

" Wisdom requires vigilance. It is a constant act of faith."

Q: Are you open to spiritual guidance?

_____

_____

_____

_____

_____

_____

> "Throughout history there have been many legends of wise souls, masters and teachers like The Hermit."

_____

_____

_____

_____

Ancient Wisdom—Color the Hermit

X—THE WHEEL OF FORTUNE

Path of: Opportunity
Ruler: Jupiter

In life we cannot avoid change, we cannot avoid loss. Freedom and happiness are found in the flexibility and ease with which we move through change.

—The Buddha

The wheel is an ancient symbol for life itself. Each turn represents a passage of time, a new stage, and as the wheel progresses, a series of experiences unfold one after another. The Wheel of Fortune could be described as the very game of life, bringing to mind a roulette wheel and other games of chance. Here, we must be willing gamblers, ready to throw the dice or chance the wheel—to play the game or allow it to play us. The name of the game is change.

The letters TARO inscribed on the wheel may be read as ROTA, which is Latin for wheel, or TORA (Torah), signifying the Hebrew law. The Wheel of Fortune is the Wheel of Law representing the natural law of constant change. Nature is a perfect example: We experience the cycles of nature with each change of season. Each phase marks a period of time and holds a different quality of experience. On this path, we are asked to embrace the idea that change is life and life is change.

Jupiter, the biggest planet in our solar system (11 times the size of Earth), rules The Wheel. In astrology, Jupiter represents expansion and is known to be an extremely positive force. Astrologers often refer to it as the good luck planet. Jupiter functions through inspiration and its expansive energy represents a need to grow and explore new horizons. A simple definition of this card is *embracing possibility*. Opportunity is all around us, and in The Wheel of Fortune, we aspire to become brave enough to explore all of our options. Success depends upon the ability to make the most of all opportunities.

This card has been called The Wheel of Karma (or Fate), symbolizing the soul as it revolves through eternity. It turns and we are born, turns again and we die, another turn and we are born again. Karma is based on the law of cause and effect, that for every action there is a consequence. The opportunity presented in The Wheel of Fortune is the willingness to learn lessons so we save ourselves from repeating them again and again.

What makes The Wheel of Fortune spin? Duality, as the principal of polarity, of opposing yet equal forces: contraction and expansion, death and rebirth, negative and positive. This stimulation of opposites results in a counter exchange of energy, which becomes perpetual motion. This can translate into both highs and lows. To calm these extremes and achieve centeredness in your life, focus on the center of the wheel. The center of the wheel is who you are now, the present you can affect. The outside of the wheel represents the unknown future with all of your fears, concerns, and stresses regarding it.

Albert Einstein once famously remarked: "God does not play dice with the universe." From a spiritual perspective, there are no accidents in life. What may seem to be luck, good or bad, could be interpreted as destiny, just as coincidence could be defined as serendipity as the gods or a larger force at work, putting us exactly where we need to be at exactly the right moment. Even so, we are all ultimately responsible for our destinies, which are determined by the choices we make every day.

The Wheel of Fortune is represented by the number 10, symbolizing the completion of a cycle and the unfolding of a new one. In numerology, one plus zero (or 10) equals one, reminding us of The Magician (as his number is one). Both The Magician and The Wheel of Fortune are cards of manifestation, and what was begun on The Magician's path comes full circle here. Sometimes it is easier to focus on what is new, because it's exciting and different, yet it is important to finish what we started (even if it does not turn out to be everything we expected)—to harvest one's crop before new seeds are planted.

The stabilizing influence in this card is the Egyptian sphinx sitting motionless above the wheel. The Sphinx is the guardian to the gateway of the mysteries of life and death. Legend says that all who passed its threshold were required to answer a riddle or be destroyed. The riddle: "What walks on four legs in the morning, two legs at noon, and three legs in the afternoon?" The answer of course is man himself, another reminder that in the journey of life, the only constant is change.

DIVINATION

Hang on to your hat because The Wheel of Fortune can be like a roller coaster ride. At the very least, life will not be boring. Here, flexibility is the key in all matters. You may feel like life is moving very quickly, forcing you outside of your comfort zones. This may translate to a feeling of being out of control. You cannot avoid change; instead make it work for you by focusing on the positive elements. Be grateful for all opportunities. It is up to you to make the most of them, even if it means extending yourself beyond old parameters. When overwhelmed, keep this perspective in mind: Do not to get stuck on what you cannot change. Instead, learn what you can and move on. This will free you to experience new opportunities.

Q: Are you open to change?

> *Hang on to your hat, the Wheel of Fortune can be like a roller coast ride!*

Q: In what areas of your life do you need to trust the greater flow?

_____

_____

_____

_____

_____

_____

_____   *" Opportunity is all*
around us, be brave
_____   *enough to explore all*
your options."
_____

_____

_____

_____

_____

_____

Ancient Wisdom—Color the Wheel of Fortune

XI—JUSTICE

Path of: Balance
Ruler: Libra

It is not only the judges at tribunals who judge; everyone judges in the degree to which he thinks. All of us, in so far as we are thinking beings, are judges.

—Anonymous, Meditations on the Tarot

In the 11th Arcanum, we meet Lady Justice. Her number is significant because it represents the mid-way point in our journey through the twenty-two pathways of the Tarot deck. The Justice Card signals a time to evaluate our experiences thus far and reflect on the possibilities ahead. Justice wears the robes of a judge and sits in judgment of our very deeds and actions. Yet she is a fair ruler. Holding a scale, the universal symbol of law and truth, she indicates that she is honored to give a fair and balanced perspective. This card represents our inner-judge, and in the best sense, the ability to see our lives from a balanced viewpoint.

In Egyptian mythology she is Maat, the Goddess of Truth and Justice. On Judgment Day, Maat took the form of an ostrich feather in the underworld as souls passed from one incarnation into another. Upon death, one's heart is said to be placed on a scale, weighed against Maat's feather on the opposite side. Until the soul's heart becomes as light as her feather, it must repeat its earthbound journey. It is one's heart, not the mind, which is judged and determines the outcome of one's worthiness to proceed forward into the next phase of the journey.

The heart is a symbol for the center. The ancients saw it as the seat of human intelligence, calling the heart the "center of illumination." To the Egyptians, it was the indispensable center of the body in eternity. In Justice, we strive to find our center, a process involving a balance of the mind and heart. A simple definition of this card is *I think and I pray*.

Symbolizing truth, fairness, and justice, Libra, the sign of the scales, rules the Justice card. Libra is an Air sign, indicating an emphasis on the intellect; this sign loves to reason and measure, a process of weighing and balancing different sides of a situation. Justice is sometimes referred to as the great orator, debating two sides of a situation to discern the truth of the matter. Yet the desire for fairness can be a double-edged sword, as the ability to see opposite sides of a situation can sometimes lead to indecision. As we evolve through life, so will our perception of truth. Justice is shown seated between two pillars; they represent severity and mercy. She offers the grace that comes from the balance of the two. In Justice, we become supreme diplomats with the ability to embrace two different perspectives and ultimately find the middle way to peace.

In astrology, Saturn is exalted in Libra as the best expression of this sign. Saturn represents Karma and the Divine Law, reminding us of the previous Arcanum, The Wheel of Fortune. Karma is the law of cause and effect. From a spiritual perspective, it is the weighing of our actions against circumstances. In some decks, this card is called "Adjustment," representing the aspects of one's life that may need adjustment. The true state of nature is balance and individual harmony is sought one way or another, whether consciously or unconsciously. This card offers the opportunity for a mid-course correction, the ability to right our ways and past indiscretions. Thus on can regain one's center and inner-equilibrium, leading to a sense of balance.

On a mundane level, this card represents the law, which can translate to legal proceedings. This may take the form of arbitration, mediation, or the signing of contracts. In all matters, The Justice card says this is a time to be precise in your actions, to dot your "i's" and cross your "t's," to make sure your affairs are in order before proceeding onto the next experience.

Justice holds a sword—the sword of truth—reminding us of the Minor Arcana's Ace of Swords. In the Tarot, Aces represent rebirth and new beginnings, here representing a time where we may need to cut away aspects of our lives that are no longer truthful or meaningful. Although Justice encourages moderation and restraint, there are times when extreme situations require extreme measures. In this process, frankness and honest exchanges, although difficult and sometimes painful, will lead to a new sense of truth.

DIVINATION

The Justice card represents a time to focus on the aspects of your life that are out of balance. During this time, you may have the ability to see both sides of a situation. Don't let this confuse you. This is a process of finding clarity that will help you find your sense of centeredness. Whenever possible, seek middle ground and resist going to extremes. Even if circumstances may appear to be unjust, abstain from righteous thought and action. Instead ask that divine truth be revealed to you. You can avoid major upheaval by doing this. However, if something in your life is severely out of balance, know that the natural course of events will be for the situation to right itself. The outcome will mirror the degree of imbalance. In any case, the truth at the heart of the matter will be found, and ultimately, you can expect a renewed sense of harmony in your life.

Q: What areas of your life are out of balance?

> *Ask that Divine Truth be revealed to you."*

Q: What adjustments do you need to make to find a greater sense of wholeness?

_____
_____
_____
_____
_____
_____
_____
_____

"*I think and I pray.*"

_____
_____
_____
_____
_____
_____

Ancient Wisdom—Color Justice

XII—THE HANGED MAN

Path of: Surrender
Ruler: Neptune
Element: Water

God grant me the serenity to accept the things I cannot change, the courage to change the things I can, and the wisdom to know the difference.

—Serenity Prayer

At first glance, The Hanged Man may seem confused, comical even, as he hangs upside down from a tree. Your instinct may be to turn him right side up and relieve his unfortunate condition. Do not be deceived. The Hanged Man is not a victim of circumstance. He has chosen this state of being. The Hanged Man shares the non-conformist nature of The Fool and presents a similar paradox: Is he completely mad or inspired by a higher calling? The Hanged Man indeed hangs from a tree, not by his neck, which would force death, but by one of his feet. In a sense, this path prepares us for the next Arcanum, Death. It is a practice run, a test, the beginning of the end to old beliefs.

The Hanged Man's heart is in the right place. He is upside down because he desires a different outlook on life. He has placed his feet in the air, the realm of spirit, because he seeks a more spiritual view: a reversal of ordinary consciousness. This card represents the need for a different attitude, a change in one's vision or perception, here representing a letting go of old material concerns and attachments. An analogy would be if you were to stand on your head and everything in your pockets (coins, etc.) would fall out. This symbolizes the release of all obstacles to achieving a higher state of awareness.

The Hanged Man looks like he is in a yoga pose, in a sense defying gravity. Yoga represents the union of spirit and self, a fitting description for this card. He is in a state of suspension, trance, or meditation. The Hanged Man is a channel (or connection) between the personality and the higher self. His is a meditation of love, a process of learning compassion for self and for others. The act of forgiveness, of letting yourself and the world off the hook, can lead to a kinder and gentler self. A simple definition of this card is *to surrender without defeat*. This means that you accept your innate right to feel well.

This card brings to mind the Greek myth of Sisyphus. The gods punished Sisyphus, the King of Corinth, for unintentionally betraying their secrets. Thus he was resigned to Hades and forced to roll a large stone uphill. It always rolled down again, a discouraging fate to say the least. There can be a punishing element to this card, a feeling, not always rational, of somehow having "displeased the gods," of feeling guilty without reason. This can manifest itself as a need to make things right, to gain redemption. Here one must be aware of becoming overly involved in drama, no matter how divine. The remedy is to surrender to God's will without becoming melodramatic in the process.

The planetary ruler for the Hanged Man is Neptune, in mythology, the god of the Sea. The element of Water here represents the universal ocean, the realm where all things merge or dissolve into one. In Neptune's healing waters we aspire to return to Source, the creative void from which all life emerged. Neptune's influence may result in the unconscious desire to want to return home, to the place where we are one and at peace. A dangerous effect of this need can be the inclination to check out, to not participate in life. Neptune represents the unconscious, the universal soul, and the deepest layers of the individual. It is our inner connection to spirit. In a healthy sense, it is the expression of one's spirituality in life and in our interactions with others.

This card may also bring to mind a crucifixion, images of martyrs as they sacrifice for humanity. Often historically, there has been a fine line between sacrifice and martyrdom. Originally the word sacrifice meant, "to make sacred." It was not to give up but to gain sanctuary. There are many fine lines on this path. For example, does The Hanged Man represent a sinner or a saint? He is, as we are, human, and thus embodies the qualities of both extremes. On this path, we experience the paradox of the two and ultimately the truth lies somewhere in between.

DIVINATION

Do not beat yourself up about things that are outside of your control. Instead let go and let be. This is a time to put your trust in a higher source (or power) to resolve that which you cannot. You may experience the feeling of being completely discouraged one moment and completely inspired the next. This is the paradox of The Hanged Man. He represents the human condition, our experience as we strive to make a better life for those around us and ourselves. If your actions are based on guilt, then you may not be in alignment with your higher self. Here you do not have to make amends. However, this is not a time for complacency. Escapism, though a tempting consideration, is not your best option. When all else fails, evoke love. Leave behind mortal melodrama and find your sacred connection.

Ancient Wisdom—Journal the Hanged Man

Q: Are you willing to "let go and let God?"

❝ *This is a time to put your trust in a higher source to resolve that which you cannot.*"

Q: What does surrender mean to you?

_____

_____

_____

_____

_____

_____

> *"To surrender without defeat."*

_____

_____

_____

_____

_____

_____

Ancient Wisdom—Color the Hanged Man

XIII—DEATH

Path of: Endings
Ruler: Scorpio

Why are people so afraid of death? The answer is simple. It is an unknown experience.
—James Van Praagh

Death appears here on horseback, in the guise of a dark knight. He is Cronos, Saturn, or Father Time, and he waits ready to transport us from one existence to another, an experience that could be described as the ultimate journey into the unknown. At this moment one may ask: Why me? Why now? It is important to state up front that the Death card rarely represents a physical death. Instead, this card symbolizes a death of a more subjective nature, an end to old attachments that have outlived their purpose in our lives.

This card is ruled by Scorpio, the sign of the Zodiac representing death and rebirth, and symbolizing profound transformation. Scorpio is ruled by Pluto, also known as Hades, the Lord of the Underworld. The underworld is a metaphor for the unconscious mind. Scorpio is a Water sign. In the highest sense, the element of Water represents the spirit or soul, and on a more mundane level, the emotional body.

The transformation represented in the Death card is often of an emotional or psychological nature, involving habits, compulsions, attachments, and desires that lie beneath the surface and negatively affect the quality of our day-to-day lives. The underworld is an easy place to get stuck. Yet, the scorpion has the power to transform into an eagle and fly higher than any other bird. This transformation represents the ability to experience life from a higher or more spiritual perspective.

The Winter Solstice is the symbolic death of the calendar year. With winter comes an opportunity for reflection, a time where the earth sleeps before it is reborn again in spring. Cronos (or Death) is often portrayed as a skeleton with a scythe, harvesting the old grain so it can become seed and regenerate, symbolizing the natural transition of life, here meaning a clearing away of the old to make ready for the new.

The French call sleep le petite mort, "the little death." This reminds us that we die everyday, in many different ways, and that in the span of a lifetime we experience many psychological changes. The common denominator in all things, death, birth, love, sex, or sleep, is that we are forced to relinquish control. A simple definition of this card is *letting go*. By releasing the past, you will be free to live again. Pain and suffering come from holding onto old ways of being.

The earth is the temporal plane, meaning life is temporary, a brief and fleeting moment in time. On this path, we come face to face with our mortality. Ultimately, death can give birth to a desire for a deeper meaning in life. The Death card represents a need to relinquish control, a renewed and compelling need to live more fully and value each moment.

A spiritual belief system (no matter its form) helps in navigating this path—the faith to believe that the universal plan does not give us any more than we can handle. When faced with big changes, we are forced to explore and to define our current priorities. The mystics say that within the mystery of life is an understanding of death.

Some cultures celebrate death. For example, in Latin America, the "Day of the Dead" festival acknowledges the dead and celebrates the soul's journey into another world. Theirs is a celebration of the natural cycle of life and death, a tradition that comes with dancing skeletons. The message being that by embracing death, we embrace life, and that fearing death only limits the fullest experience of life.

Dr. Elisabeth Kübler-Ross, the famous pioneer of studies on death and dying, describes the final stage of death as acceptance, that by surrendering oneself to death, there is the possibility of some peace. Ross writes, from personal experience: "The only thing that lives forever is love." Unconditional love for self transforms death into a journey of possibilities.

DIVINATION

This is a time to breathe. Inhale and take in the new breath of life, then exhale and release the past and the old energy that has outlived its purpose. The Death card represents a time of profound change—change that will transform your life. In the process, you may experience a sense of deep loss, leaving you feeling emotionally raw and vulnerable. Grief is a natural and important part of honoring any death. To help you move on, a ritual may be in order. This could be in the form of an altar, to symbolically bring to closure what you are letting go of. Or perhaps you could try a burning ritual, where you burn old remnants of the past and release them into a greater good. Most importantly, creating time for your spiritual practice will help bring you peace. As always, time will heal all wounds. For now, mourn your endings and celebrate the new beginnings ahead.

Q: What areas of your life need to "die", so new life can begin?

> *" Grief is an important part of honoring any death."*

Q: Are you willing to let go of old behaviors that no longer serve you?

" On this path we come face to face with our mortality."

Ancient Wisdom—Color Death

113

XIV—TEMPERANCE

Ruler: Sagittarius
Path of: Alchemy

Through art (the process of learning) the whole mass of base metals (the mental body of ignorance) was transmuted into pure gold (wisdom), for it was tinctured with understanding.

—Manly P. Hall

Ancient alchemy was not only a science, but also a philosophy and a religion. Initiation into the *Great Work*, as alchemy was called, required direction of the mind towards an understanding of the elements of nature (human and all other) and their connection to the Divine. The participant could only understand the essence of the alchemical experiment by active participation in the process, with different levels depending on the initiate's experience. Temperance, like alchemy, represents a learning ground where you, the initiate, become a full participant in understanding the interaction of different elements in your life and how they may ultimately direct and influence its course. This is both a lofty and worthwhile endeavor, for the realization of the different ingredients in life provides the very recipe for wisdom.

The image of the Temperance card is dominated by the presence of a mighty angel. He is the Great Omnipresent Guardian Angel looking out for our best interests and protecting us on our journey through the Tarot deck. By choosing to enter into its mysteries, we are exposed to many dangers. Knowledge, whether too much or too little, can prove harmful without a foundation of earnest and beneficial intent. The guardian angel watches over us as we aspire to participate in this knowledge toward the attainment of true wisdom. His presence is an essential component of this path. Without the guiding influence of a higher order and purpose there could only be intellectual or ego gratification.

Sagittarius, the sign of the Zodiac representing higher wisdom, rules the Temperance card. Sagittarius, shooting his arrows into the sky, is the sign of the archer and the huntsman. The arrows are of directed will, representing the desire to reach into the realm of the gods in the hunt to experience the highest levels of wisdom. Sagittarius is also a centaur, the mythological creature with the lower body of horse and the upper body of a man. This sign represents the transformation of our base animal nature into the ability of the human mind to perceive and to think. Through temperance, we aspire to self-restraint. Here wisdom, the ability to synthesize experience into reason, is the great equalizer. This card translates to wisdom through experience, for without an understanding of different experiences in life we are left to the plane of simple ignorance.

The sign opposite of Sagittarius is Gemini, the ruler of The Lovers card. Temperance and The Lovers are complimentary paths because both focus on learning though experience. In The Lovers, it is Cupid that directs the course of the arrow, piercing through the lover's blissful ignorance and transforming it into practical knowledge. It was on this path that we first encountered the alchemical marriage. In The Lovers, this marriage represented the partnership with self, as well as with other, which transpired into a deeper understanding of one's true self. In Temperance, the interpretation is somewhat different. Here the alchemical marriage symbolizes the relationship between the elements of one's nature transformed into a greater understanding of the divinity within.

The Temperance card represents the combining of opposites, just as alchemy is a combination of both magic and science. The angel is seen pouring a liquid between two vessels: One is Fire (the sun) and the other is Water (the moon). In theory, these elements cannot combine, as each would extinguish the other. Here it is important to note that the alchemist's method of turning lead (or base metals) into gold was not only a material process, but also a symbolic and spiritual endeavor. In Temperance, Fire becomes Water and Water becomes Fire, combining together into a new state of being. This is a process of transmutation and synthesis. The previous Arcanum, Justice, represented the middle path of balance between two extremes; here it is the synthesis of both. A simple definition of this card is *The integration of opposites*.

The ancient alchemists used a crucible to combine their ingredients and Temperance is the crucible of transformation. This transformation comes about through not just one element, but in the combination of many. An analogy would be a conductor of an orchestra coordinating the different musicians and their instruments to create music together. One instrument would have only one sound, but together they achieve a symphony.

Temperance reminds us that life is the greatest experiment and the adventure comes in learning something new. In this process, one reaps the eternal treasure of golden wisdom.

DIVINATION

In Temperance, you become the alchemist, representing the ability to transform aspects of your life that need to change. This will require patience, flexibility, and self-restraint. The old adage of "what does not bend, breaks" is applicable here. Temperance may be a time where it is necessary to modify your attitude. For example, if you are angry about something, try adopting a positive attitude. You may be surprised by how a change in perspective can work to transform a situation. This path often represents the desire to expand one's knowledge, especially that of a spiritual nature. By opening yourself to learning through experience, wisdom will come to you in many different forms.

Q: Are you willing to experiment with new and different possibilities?

> " Temperance is the integration of opposites."

Q: How can you be more creative in your learning process?

___

> "Fire becomes water, water becomes fire, becoming (what is) the Alchemical Marriage."

Ancient Wisdom—Color Temperance

XV—THE DEVIL

Path of: Fear
Ruler: Capricorn

What brings us out of comfort and fear is imagination—creativity. Those who truly love danger aren't extreme athletes, triathaloners or mountaineers. Creative people plunge into disaster every time they do something new; they risk everything that's familiar to them.

—John Tarrant

In the previous Arcanum, Temperance, we met a present and forceful angel. In The Devil, we experience the angel's counterpart or shadow side. The Devil is one of the most difficult cards of the Tarot to interpret as its very presence carries many meanings and misperceptions. To fully understand this path, we must put aside superstitious images of black magic, witchcraft, and evil. Some would say there is no such thing as the devil, that it is a creation of the human imagination. In this card, The Devil is very real in the sense that it represents our inner most fears and unresolved desires. The Devil is a projection of our dark side.

We see The Devil in this card as a grotesque figure, a beast with bat wings. We first met the beast in the Strength card, representing our primal, animal nature. The Devil can represent procreative energy: the vital force fueling our sexual and creative power. Throughout time, the devil often appears as a serpent and there is usually a test accompanying his presence. Transmutation is much like a snake shedding its skin. Here we apply the art of alchemy (that is, the Temperance card), of transforming this vital energy into creative power. As in the Strength card, love is the key to a compassionate transformation.

Capricorn, an Earth sign and the sign of the goat, is the ruler of The Devil card. Representing the established order, this sign is by nature materialistic—the mountain goat with the endurance and fortitude to climb to the peaks of achievement. Often controlled, and concerned with appearance, it is the very measure of propriety. Yet Capricorn is also associated with the Greek deity Pan, the hoofed and horned god of the woodlands. Pan is a fertility god who played his magic flute and filled humans with fear, for he took away their strength by casting a spell of unrelenting lust and desire. The devil represents the earthiest component of human nature, the instincts of the body. This card signals a time where we may need to take a break from duty and responsibility: to release our inhibitions and experience our own personal Dionysian rites of divine decadence. The danger lies in going too far. Remember, by playing with fire sometimes one can get burned.

With The Devil we seek a balance between self-discipline and healthy escapism. This requires an attunement with our bodies. When our needs and desires are repressed they can turn into projected judgment, looking for a scapegoat to blame for our unresolved issues. The darkest component of The Devil is a loss of faith in ourselves and in others.

The sign of Capricorn also represents power and ambition. This card exhibits the potential for power struggles. On The Devil's path, we discover whether or not we are manipulating others for our own means. The dark side of ambition is control, to get what we want at all costs, where negative materialism—the fear of not having—begins to rule our very thoughts and actions.

Mythology tells us that Lucifer (the devil) was an angel cast out of heaven for the sin of pride, or hubris. Interestingly, the original meaning of hubris is sexual passion. Lucifer is the light bringer, the dweller of the flame. If life is hell, then we are asked to consider the possibility that we have created it. On this path, we descend into the flames in order to transform our darkness into light.

A simple definition of this card is *burning through fear*. Like the Shamanic tradition of walking on hot coals, here we fire-walk and release our fears. Meeting our dark side can result in an inner power struggle between two aspects of self—the dark and the light. We can be found wrestling with inner demons and going "mad" in the process. The dark side can represent our secret self. Make friends with it because to ignore it will surely sabotage you.

This card shows a male and female in chains, in bondage to the devil. Yet if we look closely, we see that their chains are loose; they can choose to slip out of them. Here, we are offered the choice to release ourselves from the bonds that steal our power. A good sense of humor is helpful, as laughter can break spells. Your humor can give you the ability to take a step back and laugh at the cosmic joke.

DIVINATION

An important distinction on this path is that you are not your fear. The fears you're experiencing are neon markers for the things you've been seeking to change, aspects of self that have been restricting your journey forward. Let go of such fear-based behaviors as obsession, addiction, and control. Also on the list is relinquishing judgment of self and others, thoughts like, "I'm not good enough," "he/she doesn't love me," and "I'll never have what I need." The substitution of material goods or gains to escape the journey is not your answer. Although it may feel harsh, facing your fears will transform you. Creative people take risks. Ultimately, the only thing you have to lose is your fear.

Ancient Wisdom—Journal the Devil

Q: What are your deepest fears?

___

"*Make friends with your devils, if not they will surely sabotage you.*"

Q: What is your relationship with your shadow side?

> *The Devil is very real in the sense that it represents our innermost fears and unresolved desires. The Devil is a projection of our dark side.*

Ancient Wisdom—Color the Devil

XVI—THE TOWER

Path of: Destruction
Ruler: Mars

The elders have sent me here to tell you that now is like a great, rushing river. And this will be experienced in many different ways. There are those who would hold onto the shore—there is no shore. The shore is crumbling. Push off into the middle of the river.

—Choquosh, Native American Storyteller

The Tower card presents a frightening picture. Here we see a towering fortress struck by a bolt of lightning and unwitting souls falling to their seeming demise in its fiery destruction. In some archaic decks, The Tower was called *The Lightning*, or "Le Feu du Ciel," meaning *Fire from Heaven*, bringing to mind images of biblical proportion—fire and brimstone, the punishing wrath of an angry, unsatisfied god.

Indeed, The Tower closely parallels the legendary story of "The Tower of Babel," a fable of humankind's attempt to conquer the heavens through a false system of values. The Tower of Babel symbolizes the sins of pride, conceit, and over-confidence.

What are we to make of such a card, and more importantly, its implications? First, we need a little perspective. Our world, the world we live in today, is in a sense a tower, meaning that the fundamental structures, the institutions (government, religion, law, and commerce) that humankind has created and accepted through decades and centuries of time are no longer working for us. Simply put, they have become obsolete. These decaying towers must be dismantled before a process of renewal and restoration can take place.

Gerd Ziegler, in his book *Tarot: Mirror of the Soul*, describes The Tower in this way: "Just as the extraction of a rotten tooth provides relief for the entire body, the destruction of stagnant situations and relations which hinder growth begins a healing process for your entire organism. Having a tooth extracted can be painful, but when the tooth is poisoning your system, there is no other choice."

Ancient Wisdom—Journal the Tower

A simple definition of this card is *fundamental change*. The Tower represents a test of what you value and hold to be true, what is essential to your growth and well-being. In a universal context, The Tower symbolizes the destruction of an old order so that a new order can arise. In the next Arcanum, The Star represents this prophesied new order: the manifestation of an era of enlightenment for all humanity.

On a personal level The Tower card represents a death, not in the physical sense, but in endings, extreme change, and ultimately transformation and rebirth. The Tower is external change, as compared with the Death card, which represents internal change. The Tower usually indicates an extreme shift in our outer reality, meaning the structures of our everyday life.

Mars, the fieriest of all planets (with the exception of the sun), rules The Tower. Fire represents the desire for growth, a force of energy that cannot be contained or denied. Mars is the and Destruction, here signifying purification and cleansing by fire, a need for growth at all costs. By its very nature, destruction implies chaos, and on this path, we must be willing to embrace the concept of creative chaos. It is through chaos, no matter how uncomfortable or even painful, that creativity is born and new life comes into being.

The Tower card is often associated with the mythological bird the Phoenix, representing death and renewal. According to legend, when the Phoenix saw death draw near, it would make a nest of sweet-smelling wood and resins, then expose itself to the full force of the sun's rays until it burst into flames. Another Phoenix would then arise from its ashes. This path represents the necessity of periodic destruction in our lives so that recreation and regeneration can ultimately take place.

DIVINATION

You are experiencing an extreme cycle of change requiring you to let go of old structures in your life that no longer serve you. Do not try to control or manipulate this change. Instead, trust that by letting go of the old, a new sense of order will arise. You will find it easier to go with the flow. This could be an unsettling time and you may feel like you have nothing to hold onto. Still, you must let go. When overwhelmed, pray for grace. During this period, you may experience sudden flashes of insight or perception, like a flash of lightning in a thunderstorm, clarity with glimpses of what is to come. This is not the moment for rebuilding. Rebuilding will come later. For now, cry the tears of the Phoenix and heal your wounds. This healing is an important part of the process, of you making way for the new.

Ancient Wisdom—Journal the Tower

Q: What life structures need to be dismantled so you can create anew?

_____
_____
_____
_____
_____
_____
_____

> *" It is through chaos, no matter how uncomfortable, that new life comes into being."*

Essence of the Tarot Journal and Coloring Book

Q: Where do you need to surrender and trust divine process?

___

" *From the ashes rises the phoenix.*"

Ancient Wisdom—Color the Tower

137

XVII—THE STAR

Path of: Inspiration
Ruler: Aquarius

Gather out of star-dust
Earth-dust, Cloud-dust, Storm-dust
And splinters of hail,
One handful of dream-dust
Not for sale.

—Langston Hughes

From the ruins of The Tower appears The Star, a bright and welcome light. It is no coincidence that The Star follows in The Tower's destructive wake. Through the path of The Tower, our structures and foundations were torn asunder. This restructuring occurs because the immense creative potential of The Star could never be contained within The Tower's restrictive walls. It is only *after* the tearing away of past limitations that The Star is free to shine. Here, the Phoenix rises from the ashes.

Aquarius rules The Star. The symbol for Aquarius is the "water bearer," which may be confusing, as Aquarius is an Air sign. To understand, we must take the concept of Air and expand it beyond the mundane, from the realm of the mind and the intellect into a larger sphere, through the ethers and into the realm of energy and space. Aquarius is the vessel for cosmic energy, the universal waters of consciousness, and what is sometimes referred to as the Universal or Cosmic Mind. Through The Star, we connect to the unlimited destiny of all humankind.

The woman pictured here is the goddess Nuith, Our Lady of the Stars. She holds two cups (or chalices), symbolizing the merging of two streams of consciousness: the Greater Conscious into the Individual Conscious. She pours the heavenly waters into the earth. The Star is a channel symbolizing the ancient and sacred treatise, "as above, so below." This path represents heaven on earth; it is the manifestation of the celestial into material form.

The Star is the first of the three "Luminaries" of the Tarot deck (followed by The Moon and The Sun). A Luminary is a source of light. The Star is *creative light*, or inspiration. One definition of inspiration is, "the act of drawing breath into the body." Inspiration is divine breath, the taking in of divinity and the receiving of spirit. Creativity is a gift from God and it comes from spirit. You, as the artist, in whatever form this may take, are a channel for this divine force. The artist and poet William Blake described this creative power as the imagination and said it was God itself.

A simple definition of this card is the *power of dreams*. Dreams and imagination are essential to the future of humankind. For without our innate ability to imagine, to dream, to be that small hopeful child who wishes upon a star, we would be lost to a world of the ordinary and the mundane. Through our creative mind, we become poet, artist, leader, and visionary. We are immortal, magical, and we can touch the stars.

The Star is the most encompassing card of the deck in the sense that it inspires us to cultivate largesse of spirit. The power of The Star lies in its ability to inspire greatness, not only in us, but in others as well. The Star represents creative brilliance, the ego and the personality elevated. Stars are generous with their light. They are leaders and motivators. This path encourages us to transcend our limitations and to connect to a higher purpose and vision, not only for our own sake, but ultimately, for the sake of all humanity.

Within us all lies The Star's potential. Yet manifesting one's dreams requires a great deal of faith. The Star card is often associated with the "Star of Bethlehem," symbolizing the recognition of cosmic forces greater than ourselves. These forces lead us to an unknown destiny. They also remind us of The Hermit's journey and his test of faith. With The Star, like The Hermit, we must believe enough in our power and our vision to chance the unknown and see where it will take us. In Kabalistic teachings, The Star is represented by the letter Tzaddi, meaning "fish hook." Here lies a poetic idea, that it is time to cast your line out into the great sea of imagination and see what you will catch. A fly-fisher would describe their process as both an art and a meditation. Remember, if you don't like your catch, you can always throw it back into the ocean.

DIVINATION

You are creating your future now. This is a time for expanding your vision, for opening yourself to a whole new realm of possibilities.

Think big! You are only limited by the bounds of your imagination. What inspires you? What is your dearest wish, your dream? Greatness comes from your faith to believe, especially in yourself. Trust your vision even if you are not sure where it will take you, or of its exact form. Be willing to experiment with all possibilities. Don't worry if others don't understand; you may be ahead of your time. Radiate confidence. Think of yourself as a pioneer, a shining light for others to follow. This could prove to be an exceptionally creative period for you. Dance fearlessly with your muses and let them guide you to manifesting what can be.

Ancient Wisdom—Journal the Star

Q: What is your inspiration, dearest wish, future dream?

> "As you reach for your stars, you elevate your life and become a shining light for others to follow."

Q: Are you willing to explore all possibilities?

> " *Dreams and imagination are essential to the future of all humankind.*"

Ancient Wisdom—Color the Star

XVIII—THE MOON

Path of: Darkness
Ruler: Pisces

A promise to control the tide is always a lie. The resolute moon is more persistent than the best of intentions.
—Claudia Mauro

We enter into uncharted territory through the 18th Arcanum—The Moon. These are the dark and murky waters of the subconscious, the subterranean depths of mind and soul. The Moon card is associated with what has been known to mystics for centuries as the dark night of the soul. The Moon's dark journey is one that is not always willingly taken, for at times it can be both frightening and disorienting. The Bogeyman comes in the night, and on this path we dance with inner demons and ghosts from the past. Yet for better or for worse, in darkness, we have no choice but to merge with our shadow.

The Moon card looks both sinister and alluring. Here we see a full moon ripe with secrets. Two watchtowers stand beneath it. The towers guard the threshold to an invisible world, the dark void of the unknown. On this card, a wolf and a dog are seen baying at the moon. The use of the number two is significant as it represents the dual nature of this card and reminds us of the Tarot's second Arcanum, The High Priestess and the Queen of the Moon. Moonlight can be deceptive, casting an illusory light. Here we may feel caught between two worlds, the real and the unreal.

The wolf and the dog are two aspects of The Moon. The wolf is a totem for our most basic animal instincts, representing primal psychic energy. The dog is Anubis, the Egyptian god of the underworld, and here truly man's best friend. Anubis guides lost souls through the many hidden dangers of the underworld. His presence on this card sends the important message that we do not have to be alone in this journey. We can seek help and guidance in negotiating the darkness.

Finally we see a crayfish, representing Cancer, the astrological ruler of the moon (or a dung-beetle, the Egyptian scarab that carries the sun across the horizon). The crayfish is shown rising out of a muddy pool. The pool represents unconscious waters that may have become stagnant and lifeless. The result can be an emotional stagnation, a feeling of being stuck in the deep muck of one's past.

This may lead to depression and profound despair, yet there is cause for hope. In some interpretations, the crayfish is actually a scorpion, representing Scorpio (the astrological sign of death and rebirth) and symbolizing emotional and spiritual regeneration. This signals that it is time to emerge from the depths of darkness and reach for the light. A simple definition of this card is *a soul in search of rebirth*.

The Moon is the second of the Tarot's Luminaries or "lights." It is the very act of opening ourselves to the light, as we did in "The Star," that attracts the dark. The brighter the light, the more our darkness becomes apparent. The Moon is Reflected Light, mirroring the light of the sun. The goal in this card is to go from the dark side of the moon, a place that no light can reach, to a place of reflection, which leads to illumination. Ultimately, The Moon represents the journey of enlightenment.

Pisces rules The Moon, symbolized as two fish swimming in opposite directions, and again representing a conflict between two worlds, or two realities. Pisces are sensitive creatures, greatly open to the non-physical psychic realm. Those with strong moon characteristics have a highly developed feminine nature representing the intuitive, feeling, and receptive aspects of self. This combination makes one highly attuned to unseen influences, especially the influence of other people: their emotions, needs, and projections. On this path, we must be careful not to be pulled into other people's "stuff." The Moon suggests a time for setting clear boundaries, for separating our needs from the needs of others.

This realm is a tricky one, for moonlight is always elusive and cannot be caught. Nonetheless, we must be willing to delve into the inner mystery, facing phantasms along the way. It is an understatement to say that this card offers profound wisdom, a wisdom that can only come from darkness. In the process of seeking and attaining wisdom, The Moon can be a most powerful ally.

DIVINATION

If you have chosen this card, it is time for an emotional house cleaning to clear out the cobwebs of the past, to bring to closure parts of your life that are holding you back. This may require going outside of your comfort zone as you let go of old behaviors or relationships that no longer serve you. It is easy to be caught in The Moon's spell, so here we must be careful not to become enamored or bewitched by our illusions. Spend time with your dreams-cape; in that realm you will reacquaint yourself with your deepest nature. To explore the gifts of your darkness, you may need to enter a period of hibernation. It is always darkest before the light.

Q: What do you need to resolve and let go of to move forward?

___

"*In the process of attaining wisdom, The Moon can be a most powerful ally.*"

Essence of the Tarot Journal and Coloring Book

Q: Where do you need to set different boundaries?

_____
_____
_____
_____
_____
_____
_____

" The dark night of the soul."

_____
_____
_____

Ancient Wisdom—Color the Moon

XIX—THE SUN

Path of: Joy
Ruler: The Sun

Give forth thy light to all without doubt; the clouds and shadows are no matter for thee.
—Aleister Crowley

The Sun itself is the planetary ruler of this card. This is the first indication of the beautiful simplicity inherent to this path. The Sun card encourages us to look at the world through the eyes of a child, with purity and simplicity, without forethought to agendas or worry of outcomes. Gazing upon the bright imagery of this card, one cannot help but feel a sense of optimism and joy. Just as the sun rises in the east and sets in the west, with each new morning, with each light of day, we experience an awakening—a rebirth. In The Moon, we encountered the dark and sleepy illusions of night. In The Sun, we experience the clarity that comes from one who has been reborn. The Sun symbolizes the beginning of a brand new day.

The Sun is the center of our solar system, and all planets orbit around it. It is our brightest and fieriest star. Through The Sun card, we connect to the need to shine, the desire to be seen and to express one's own unique self, one's own light. The sun is a symbol for our life force—the divine spark of self—our true essence. In astrology, the sun represents the light of the personality, which is in a state of constant evolution as we experience life. The personality, with all of its unique and colorful nuances, is the vehicle for the expression of one's self in this lifetime. The anchor for self is the ego. Often the ego gets a bad rap, seen as vain or selfish. Yet, without your ego, there would be no focus for the light.

The Sun is dynamic and magnetic, a powerful source. It is no wonder then that since antiquity the sun has been worshiped as a supreme deity representing great power and strength. The astrological symbol for the sun is a circle with a dot in the middle, ultimately representing wholeness. When self-expression comes from a place of centered-ness and well-being, it is a truly magnificent sight to behold. It becomes sheer joy—the freedom and exhilaration of expressing one's self. A simple definition of this card is *enthusiasm*.

The Sun completes the trinity of the Tarot's Luminaries, representing Revealed Light. The Sun presents freedom. This is a freedom from not only one's personal and emotional past (The Moon), but also on a deeper level from past karmic cycles. In the highest sense, there is no "baggage" on this path. The result is that here we have nothing to hide. The Sun offers the freedom to reveal ourselves, to share our light without concern about what others may think or how we will be received, what could be described as a release of all expectation. Robert Wang, in *The Qabalistic Tarot*, describes The Sun as a *new innocence*. He writes, "It is, quite literally, a growing younger, a process of birth backwards until we reach a stage where there is some recollection of the source from which we emerged."

The energy of The Sun is transformative. In alchemy, the sun (or sulfur) is an important ingredient in the symbolic process of transforming lead into gold. The heat of the sun ignites within us a positive force, a purifying influence that can turn the most base of matter into something precious and beautiful. Through this path, we experience the "golden touch" in all endeavors, hence The Sun's traditional definition: *success!*

If there is a challenge in The Sun, then it is a happy one: adjusting to enjoyment and taking pleasure in your newfound success. We live in a complicated world and today's society has become acclimated to an unhealthy diet of worry and stress. It is easy to get caught up in all the hustle and bustle of life, the pressure to be busy, hurry, get ahead, and solve all your problems. The message of The Sun is simple: *Don't worry, be happy.*

DIVINATION

Here are seven steps to embracing the successful essence of The Sun.

1. Live your life in the present.

2. Experience each moment fully. Look around you to see and feel the wonders of all creation.

3. Pretend that you do not have a care or worry in the world.

4. Be like a child whose only agenda is to simply be, to play and frolic in the light of the sun.

5. When experiencing a problem or dilemma trust that by letting go, it will be resolved in a beneficial way.

6. Be active. Whenever possible, say "yes." Why? Because you can.

7. Then, and most importantly, become the light and shine your magnificent presence unto the world. Your mantra now: everyday, in every way, my life gets better and better.

Ancient Wisdom—Journal the Sun

Q: Are you ready to shine your light?

_____

_____

_____

_____

_____

_____

_____

_____

❝ *When self-expression comes from a place of centeredness, it is a magnificent sight to behold.*"

_____

_____

_____

_____

Essence of the Tarot Journal and Coloring Book

Q: How can you live your life more joyfully?

_____
_____
_____
_____
_____
_____
_____

"Whenever possible say 'Yes!' Why? Because you can!"

_____
_____
_____
_____
_____

Ancient Wisdom—Color the Sun

XX—JUDGMENT

Path of: Reckoning
Ruler: Pluto
Element: Fire

Prayer is an egg.
Hatch out
the total helplessness
inside.

—Rumi

The image portrayed in this card is of the biblical "Last Judgment," also known as the Day of Reckoning. By definition, reckoning means to deal with, the settlement of accounts. Simply stated, it is accountability. There comes a moment in life where one is forced to look into the harsh mirror of reality, where illusion and pretension are stripped away and one comes face to face with what is the true self. This moment is the essence of the Judgment card. This is the end of your world, or at least some part of it, as you currently know it.

Yet, the Judgment card is not a death sentence, although in the moment it may very well seem that way. In fact, this card represents just the opposite. Through the path of Judgment, there is opportunity. There is the potential for a renewal, an awakening of such magnitude that it may be overwhelming to comprehend and, in the beginning, difficult to incorporate. But before we deal with the rebirth inherent to this card, we must first address the death.

The ruler for the Judgment card is Pluto. In astrology, this planet symbolizes death and rebirth. On a mundane level, this means change and growth. On a higher level, Pluto is the soul in its experience of transformation. Transformation can sometimes be painful, for it is often stimulated by crisis. Without the crisis, we would not be forced to deal with the changes that are necessary to our growth. Pluto is truth, in the sense of a naked soul stripped to its very essence, an experience that could be described as "meeting your maker" totally exposed.

The element for Judgment is Fire. Fire is the creative life force; it is the purest expression of free will. Fire is inherently growth oriented and it can be intense in its desire for change. The element of Fire can have a purifying effect, burning away the past to give rise to the future. In Judgment, it represents a baptism by fire. This path lets you choose between rebirth and death, Heaven and Hell. It asks, "If you were to die today, what would be your regrets? Did you walk your talk? Did you speak your truth?" These are intimidating questions, questions that boil down to personal integrity.

Don't panic. Notice the angel so magnificently pictured here. He is the Archangel Michael, the leader of the forces of light and the sun, symbolizing rebirth. It is said that Michael routed the devil and hosts of darkness in the war of Heaven. He blows a trumpet, calling souls to rebirth. Richard Cavendish, in his book on the Tarot, quotes Michael's message as, "We can rise from the grave of our old dead self now, while we are still in the physical body, if our ears are not deaf to the trumpet call from on high."

To quote the Buddha, "There is only one time when it is essential to awaken. That time is now." The Judgment card is a call to action. It is never too late to make change, and now more than ever. This card represents a turning point in consciousness; a point where personal will aligns with the higher soul in a quest for truth. A simple definition of this card is *conscious rebirth*. The result is a more profound and honest reality.

The Judgment card requires a critical analysis of your life, a facing of facts. In this process, it is easy to get caught up in black and white thinking—good vs. bad. But on a higher level, there is no such thing as right or wrong. Essentially the whole point of "Judgment" is to not judge. Your life and your processes are between you and your God, or higher self, and the same goes for others. The purpose here is not to condemn, but to inspire one to make changes for a higher good. Ultimately in the Judgment, severity is subdued, giving way to hope and to mercy. On this path, we are encouraged toward tolerance, not only for ourselves, but also for those around us. It is said that unless you have walked in someone else's shoes, you cannot truly understand their journey. In honoring your own choices, you can then honor the choices of others.

DIVINATION

The Judgment card represents a wake-up call, a time to commune with your higher self. Now is the moment for a reassessment of your life. To make amends and bring into settlement any old or unresolved issues, accounts, or relationships. Your newfound consciousness is not an excuse to judge yourself. Remember, hindsight is always 20/20. Instead, congratulate yourself on your willingness to see your life from a more universal perspective. By taking care of outstanding matters, you will be free to experience your world in a way that is nothing short of rejuvenating. You are never helpless if you have the ability to change. Finally, at the end of the day, ask yourself: "Did I do the best that I could today?" If the answer is yes, then sing a triumphant Hallelujah, thank the powers that be, and be at peace with yourself— truly at peace.

Ancient Wisdom—Journal Judgement

Q: How do you judge yourself, others?

> *"The Judgment card represents a wakeup call, a time to commune with your higher self."*

Q: Are you standing in your truth?

> "There is only one time when it is essential to awaken. That time is now."
> —The Buddha

Ancient Wisdom—Color Judgement

XXI—THE WORLD

Path of: Wholeness
Ruler: Saturn

Honor the past as your teacher, honor the present as your creation, and honor the future as your inspiration.
—Crow, Medicine Cards

The World card represents the completion of our journey through the Tarot deck. This card is a synthesis of all paths before it, representing the accumulation of all the lessons that we have learned along the way. Now we must leave home and our inner exploration and venture into the outer world of form. Take all that we know and translate it into actual experience. When we get to The World, we have attained the wisdom and the tools necessary to create a reality that reflects our highest and truest selves. Here, the ever-evolving dream of all that we can be is finally within our grasp.

The ruler of The World card is Saturn. In astrology, this planet denotes boundaries and structure. On a physical level, it is the body, most specifically the skeletal structure, the inner foundation that shapes and defines our outer physical form. On a spiritual level Saturn symbolizes the earth's learning ground, the school of the soul. Saturn can be a hard taskmaster, for it teaches us our limitations. In ancient times, Saturn was Cronos, Father Time, representing our limited time on earth. In The World, we gain clarity about what we want to achieve in this time, defining our purpose in life. The World is the outer manifestation of this intention, relating to our career. We create an identity that others can recognize, and hopefully respect. On this path, we build our body of work in the world.

A simple definition of this card is *worldly success*. Experience the success that you have earned—that you deserve. Ultimately, The World represents the ability to be confident and proud of our accomplishments, but not arrogant. As we express our unique potential, the gifts that we were born with, we can inspire others to claim their own unique talents and abilities.

In the first Arcanum, The Magician, we realized the power of creative free will. The World is a mastery of the creative process of manifestation. Here we step into reality and realize that the life we experience is, for the most part, our own creation. In a sense, we grow up and become adults. We become empowered by embracing responsibility for creating the world that we live in. This encompasses our worlds, big and small, personal and universal. It is the balance of a bigger consciousness, the divine plan with individual free will.

The World is a completion, yet we still have much to learn. Here we have a sense of our destiny, but its full meaning has yet to unfold. Now we can only discover its meaning by experiencing ourselves in the world. This will be a process of being separate and self-sufficient, yet at the same time a part of a whole picture.

The World card shows what looks to be a female dancer balancing in the center of the world. In older decks, the figure is actually a hermaphrodite, representing male and female qualities in perfect balance. The World symbolizes what the mystics describe as the alchemical marriage or union of male and female energy, the exquisite dance of Yin and Yang that leads us into an energetic wholeness.

We, as physical beings, are made of energy. This energy is regulated by the life force, the organic substance that defines matter. This life force evolves as we move through time, our very movements activating an energy field that creates the atmosphere. The World asks us to look at the energy that we send out into the universe. The rule of "like attracts like" is important here: Whatever you put out will come back to you. In a positive sense, The World is coming into harmony with the earth flow.

The World card is a process of redefining our boundaries, a time where we expand our current structures to encompass a more worldly view. On a mundane level, this may translate to travel, to exploring the world at large. Here we become citizens of the world with the desire to pass on what we know and participate in a larger global consciousness.

DIVINATION

Now is a time to take all that you have learned into the world. You have just graduated from the School of Life. Confidence is your calling card, so don't be shy about celebrating your accomplishments. This is not showing off, but announcing your presence to the world in a positive way. You deserve acknowledgment. This card represents expansion and new opportunities, especially in regards to your career. The world is your oyster, but you are asked to take responsibility for what happens next. It is up to you. This is a time to step up to the plate and go to bat for what you believe. You are in a dance of creation and manifestation. Be clear about the energy you send out, because it will define the measure of success that you receive.

Q: What is your definition of success?

> "You are in a dance of creation and manifestation."

Q: Are you ready to boldly share your gifts with the world?

" The World is your oyster!"

Ancient Wisdom—Color the World

ABOUT THE AUTHOR

Megan Skinner received her first deck of Tarot Cards when she was fourteen years-old, beginning a compelling and lifelong adventure into the realm of mysticism, symbols and archetypes, psychic and spiritual consciousness. Today, Megan is a professional clairvoyant, Tarot card expert, astrologer and author, with a private practice in spiritual counseling for over twenty-five years.

Megan graduated from Washington State University with a Bachelor of Arts degree in Communications. She began a career in advertising, climbing the corporate ladder to become a successful account executive with a prominent Seattle advertising agency. Finding her corporate life unfulfilling, she felt called to change direction, and follow her growing love of the Tarot, astrology and spiritual awareness to help others understand their lives from a greater and deeper perspective.

In addition to *Essence of the Tarot: Journal and Coloring Book*, she is the author of *Essence of the Tarot: Modern Reflections on Ancient Wisdom*, *The Complete Idiot's Guide to Sextrology*, *Compass: Navigating Your Intuitive Gifts for Success and Wellbeing*, and most recently, her own Tarot deck: The *Couture Tarot Deck and Guidebook*.

Megan lives in Seattle, Washington. You can find out more about her and her work, and order her books and Tarot deck at MeganSkinner.com.

www.ingramcontent.com/pod-product-compliance
Lightning Source LLC
Chambersburg PA
CBHW081154070526
44583CB00021B/2826